How Did I Get Here?

My Journey Through Prostitution, Drugs, Relationships, & Love

Annette Smiley

authorHOUSE

AuthorHouse™
1663 Liberty Drive
Bloomington, IN 47403
www.authorhouse.com
Phone: 1 (800) 839-8640

© 2016 Annette Smiley. All rights reserved.

Edited By: India Rochelle

No part of this book may be reproduced, stored in a retrieval system, or transmitted by any means without the written permission of the author.

Published by AuthorHouse 08/25/2016

ISBN: 978-1-5246-2090-5 (sc)
ISBN: 978-1-5246-2089-9 (e)

Library of Congress Control Number: 2016912079

Print information available on the last page.

Any people depicted in stock imagery provided by Thinkstock are models, and such images are being used for illustrative purposes only. Certain stock imagery © Thinkstock.

This book is printed on acid-free paper.

Because of the dynamic nature of the Internet, any web addresses or links contained in this book may have changed since publication and may no longer be valid. The views expressed in this work are solely those of the author and do not necessarily reflect the views of the publisher, and the publisher hereby disclaims any responsibility for them.

Scripture quotations marked KJV are from the Holy Bible, King James Version (Authorized Version). First published in 1611. Quoted from the KJV Classic Reference Bible, Copyright © 1983 by The Zondervan Corporation.

In memory of First Lady Rose Jenkins. You are the lily of the valley and a bright and morning star. She was a woman I inspired to be. God created this special jewel to be a part of my life and my family's life especially my grandchildren. She was a loving spirit that was so needed in their lives. Some of the things I share in this book is horrific. Things that I went through in my life. Even though she could not imagine why people would choose such things. I know for certain she loved me and she loved me unconditionally. This beautiful woman seen in me what I could not see in myself. I thank God for her family sharing this precious jewel. November 20,1941-August 4th2016.

DEDICATION

I dedicate this to my Lord and Savior because without Him I would not have the ability to write this book.

I also dedicate this book to my two beautiful daughters Latasha, and Jinetta. Jesus is the reason we are so blessed. Everything the enemy means for evil, God will turn it around when we give our life to Him and live our lives to please him. I believe His promises over our family that all generation curses and strongholds will be broken. I love you however God loves you best.

I also dedicate this book to my dear brother Kenneth Ray Smiley who past away from cancer. He always loved me unconditionally. May he rest in peace 1956-2002.

This book is also dedicated to Eric Smiley we miss you dearly: The Bible says *"And I will restore to you the years the Locus has eaten.... Joel 2;25"*.

Contents

Dedication		vii
Acknowledgments		xi
Introduction		xiii
Chapter 1	My Fondest Memories	1
Chapter 2	School Days	5
Chapter 3	Running Into The Hands of Satan	11
Chapter 4	If Nothing Changes	15
Chapter 5	Been On This Mountain Long Enough	20
Chapter 6	If I Could Only Get A Job	25
Chapter 7	Total Surrender	30
Chapter 8	It's Time	35
Chapter 9	Transparency	42
Chapter 10	You Have to Encourage Yourself Sometimes	46
Conclusion: Luke 22:31-32		53
About the Author		57
Resources		59

ACKNOWLEDGMENTS

Giving all praise and honor and Glory to my Lord
and savior who saw fit to save a wretch like me.
I thank God for my parents Annie and Robert
Smiley. For without them I would not be here.
To my amazing Sister, Brenda Dinish and her
husband because they were always encouraging
me. They were the first two individuals that
seen in me what I could not see in myself.
There are so many small details that played a huge part
in how God began to transform my life. I could write
a story about each experience. And I thank God.
As I look back, I definitely have to acknowledge
Seattle Union Gospel Mission as part of some of my
life changing experiences while going through the
program and all the people God put in my path along
the way. Sometimes we don't understand why people
come in and out of our lives, but I do acknowledge all
of my experiences; the good and the bad. And I am
humbly thankful for everyone that played a role.

I am grateful for Don who stole my heart
and for the things he taught me.

Last but not least, I'd like to thank my Pastor and First Lady O.J Jenkins. They are second to none. They are a true picture of Christlikeness, honor, integrity, and truth. They are consistently loving me unconditionally and always speaking life into my family and me. I truly praise God for them.

I acknowledge Essance and Daisha my granddaughters they have been a huge part of me learning who I am.

INTRODUCTION

"I'd rather strive for the kind of interview where instead of me asking to introduce myself to society, society asks me to introduce myself to society."
Criss Jami

I suffered many things for many years, because of the choices I made. I have come to understand that even if I made different choices, that sometimes *different* doesn't always mean better.

Today I believe there is something more to me and I really don't like that it's taking so long for me to put the pieces together. I am certain I was created for a higher purpose.

Today I try and pay attention to the life I live. The everyday walk I take, my conversations, and my thoughts. When I do that it helps understand who I really am. Every experience I endure is a chance for me to learn and grow.

One of my reasons for writing this book is for me to receive healing. My vision is that people all over the world will read it and it would bring hope to someone. My desired outcome through these pages is for hearts to be touched. Maybe others could understand that after all the choices and the pain, Jesus loves them unconditionally.

As I began to reach out for help to change my life, I saw life through a different lens. Because of my new view, some of the layers of pain began to fall away and some of the walls of trust began to come down slowly. The biggest struggle has always been me desiring something more. There was a void that was missing from the inside of me. Love. I had never received love the way God had intended it and because of that, I had nothing to measure love by.

I believe that God has prepared me for this journey to share *"How Did I Get Here?"* and has equipped me with everything I need for this season of my life. There have been many distractions along the way that I have let hinder me. I was so encouraged as I read my sister in Christ' book, *"Chronicles of Pain"* by Sharon Blake. Her message became important to me because she used her voice to speak out about her pain and that encouraged me to continue on my journey.

"Lord, help me to follow your guidance and stay focused."

How did I get here? I felt at times that I was always learning but never really coming into the knowledge of truth. For many years I was unable to function properly because the wounds hurt. There were so much pain and offenses in my life.

One of my favorite scripture in the Bible, *31 And the Lord said, Simon, Simon, behold, Satan hath desired to have you, that he may sift you as wheat: 32 But I have prayed for thee, that thy faith fail not: and when thou art converted, strengthen thy brethren.* Luke 22:31-32.

I love this scripture because I have come to understand that this was true for my life. It has taken me many years to get here, and this is how I chose the title of this book, *"How Did I Get Here?"* The words that God spoke in this verse *"I have prayed for thee"* were so encouraging to me and should be to others because whatever the enemy meant to harm us with, God will use to strengthen us if we let him.

In my journey there was many times I wanted to give up. That was Satan sifting through me. When I was shooting up drugs in my veins, prostituting myself, stealing, lying, cheating, and leaving my children; I didn't know that strongholds were being built.

Remember God Himself said, *"I am praying for thee."* So what I knew was that someone had to be praying for me because today I am able to write this book to strengthen my brethren as I continue to go through this process of being sifted and shaken.

Today God has another purpose for my life. Every bad experience I have draws me closer to Him. For that, I am immensely grateful. Sometimes I get weary on the battlefield in my mind. However, I have a choice.

Today I understand who I am affects everything that I come in contact with. Bill Thrall, author and publisher once said, *"Vulnerability exposes the motive of our hearts to live lives of integrity and the resulting realignment of our lives convinces others of our integrity and our commitment to adhere the truth."* I needed intimacy, honesty, and healing. I knew it had to be something more. I just wanted to be cared for at the core of who I was.

What I have learned is that for true forgiveness to happen something has to die. When someone hurts you, no matter how bad it is you have to forgive him or her. Not just for them, but also for yourself. When you do that it releases something inside of you that no longer holds power over you. God will give you peace in your heart.

I have been hurt so bad that my heart felt like it was being ripped out of my chest. I have been beaten so badly with hot clothes hangers on my back that I thought I was going to die. I know I had to forgive in order to receive forgiveness.

We all have a unique destiny rooted in who we are. This book is a part of my journey of how I got here I hope this blesses your soul.

CHAPTER ONE
MY FONDEST MEMORIES

"Memories, even bittersweet ones, are better than nothing."
Jennifer L. Armentrout

My name is Annette Smiley, but my nickname was Netta. When I was a little girl my family called me *Turkey*. I believe I was named this because I was a little chubby, as a child and it didn't bother me then. But now that I am older I have learned that names are very important.

I grew up in the central area of Seattle, WA. We called it *The CD*. This area was a very beautiful neighborhood and was predominantly black in the sixties. My family moved to Seattle from Waco, Texas in 1961. I was a year old so I've always considered myself a native of Seattle. I was the youngest of eight siblings, four boys and four girls. My oldest sibling stayed in Texas. I was never sure why. Mostly because it had never been explained. I assumed he stayed behind to help out with my grandparents.

I considered my family as low middle class. My parents both worked hard and were good providers. Always making sure that we were taken care of. My mom wore the pants in our house and there was no mistake about it. No offense dad.

I was daddy's little girl. As I go down memory lane, we never ever went hungry. I can still remember all the great holidays. I loved the preparation for Easter and Christmas, the new clothes pretty dresses, ruffle socks and shiny shoes. And I especially loved the hat, purse, and the gloves to match.

I loved my hair. However, I was not fond of the process leading up to obtaining *pretty hair.* My mom could sure wash a good head. However, our hair was very thick. When it came time for the pressing comb that she used to make our hair straight and the Crisco grease, my Lord! All the sizzling and the crackling; I was never quite sure why she used cooking grease instead of hair grease. Because our hair was still damp that whole process was an adventure. But oh was it worth it. That is one of those memories and a part of our culture that can't be duplicated anywhere else.

I loved our family picnics in the summer time. We would go to *Madrone Beach* and *Lake Sammamish;* it was so much fun. But one of my other fondest memories is Halloween. My mother always got paid on the 31st of October every year. My siblings and I would be waiting and looking out the window for her car to drive up. We knew she would come inside with candy and costumes to get ready for trick or treating and to pass out candy. We always had consistency in our family.

As children, we could count on certain things from our parents. I never remember our lights being turned off or going hungry. I am sure we had struggles but they never allowed us to see it. I remember everything from the food bank we received and for that we were grateful. In that season I was a happy child.

Guardian Angels

I remember on Friday nights my parents getting ready to go out to the local bar called *Madrone Tavern*. I remember rubbing *Jergen's* lotion on my mom's legs. I will never forget that smell. I loved doing that for my mom and it seemed like it took forever to rub it in. I knew my mom and dad loved each other dearly. The piece that became confusing to me was when they left for the tavern, they were happy. It was always when they came back that they were arguing and fighting for hours. It was really bad but this was the normal routine almost every weekend for my family. It got so bad that my mother and father nearly lost their lives. As a child I began to understand that the stuff they were drinking made them feel and act different. I still couldn't understand why they did it weekly.

One of the most tragic moments was when my mom was driving home from the Tavern one night and she blacked out and ran into a pole. The car caught on fire around 2:00am that morning. Gratefully, someone pulled her out of the car. She was severely burned on different parts of her body.

There was another tragedy where my dad could have died because of them drinking alcohol and my mom could have gone to prison. As I have gotten older I see how all of this has affected me, especially the way I felt about who I was. I never knew how to talk about it to anyone so it was never talked about. I deemed it as normal and accepted it as such. I really thought this was love or part of love.

On Sundays, they would rest up and prepare for work for the rest of the week. There was never any discussion about any of the fights. They would always get back to the normal routine. I never remember any of my siblings discussing this. If they did, they didn't let me hear it. This went on for a while, but after the accident my mom stopped drinking from that point on.

CHAPTER TWO
SCHOOL DAYS

*"Wisdom is not a product of schooling but
of the lifelong attempt to acquire it."*
Albert Einstein

I remember my father taking me to pre-school. I can't remember any of my experiences in the classrooms or my teachers. I don't know why my memory is blocked from those years.

When I got in middle school, I had very few friends. My sister seemed to be very popular. Really it wasn't so much of her being popular that made others attracted it to her, but my sister had what I called *the gift of gab.* She could talk to anyone and because of that she made a lot of friends.

I always wanted *the gift of gab*, instead I was quiet and not sure about anything. I knew that something was missing but I didn't know what. I now can identify that I was insecure about who I was. I didn't know neither my identity nor that I was likeable because I measured that by the attention other girls got and the attention I didn't get.

During middle school I joined a dance group called the *African Drum Assembly*. This was huge for me because it would be the first thing that I would do where people could acknowledge me. I was dying for some attention because I didn't have an outlet. No one ever pulled that out of me or even ask me what I was feeling or how I was doing. I think because I was quiet everyone thought I was ok. And as a child, what could I possibly be going through at such a young age? If anyone had reached out to me with tender love and care, I would have latched on like a magnet.

My summer before starting high school, there was this one family that moved in across the street from us. Aunt Gussie and Uncle Leo is what I came to know them as. They were the most loving people I had known and above all else, they loved people unconditionally. My parents didn't like me hanging out at their house because it seemed like a lot of people would be over there. The cars that were parked outside were Cadillac Eldorado's; cars hustlers drove. My parents believed anyone driving these types of cars and who wore certain types of clothes and flashy jewelry were hustlers, drug dealers, or pimps. The women that hung on their arms were so pretty and they were nice. Aunt Gussie use to play cards with her friends and I began to help her by babysitting when she would have games at her house. I would help sell soda pops and food and she would pay me. I found out later that her son was a pimp and there were hustlers in and out. What I didn't understand is how she still loved him unconditionally.

I started my first year of high school at Garfield High. This should have been an exciting time, but for me it wasn't. I didn't have a lot of friends. I only had one best friend and my cousins. This was the year I tried smoking weed; I didn't like it. Personally, I just wanted to fit in. I remember the school looking so big to me and the hallways being dark. I really felt like I didn't belong there. There were different sets of girls and I didn't seem to fit it in with any of them. It didn't take long for me to begin to make the wrong choices.

Choices

This one boy, that I didn't know was popular at the time, had a girlfriend on the cheerleading team. I was scared and happy when I noticed he was paying attention to me, but all he wanted was to have sex with me.

There was always talk about guys talking about who would be the first one in their group of friends that could sleep with the new freshman girl. He actually had a bet with his friends and that's exactly what happened. I never even talked to him after that. I was only 14 years old. To this day I don't know how I got pregnant it was less than 30 seconds; I am not saying this to be mean or throw shade, but it really was.

Months had gone by and I realized I hadn't gotten my period and then my stomach began to grow. I was getting bigger and bigger. I was petrified! There was no one I could talk to and there was no way I could tell my family.

I continued to go to school. I would stay behind to get dressed since me and my big sister shared a room.

One day my sister forgot something and came back into the room just as I was changing my shirt. My sister walked in and in that moment I realized how big I was.

My poor sister was in disbelief looking at her baby sister with this huge stomach and of course she told my parents. This was I think one of the worst things I experienced as a young child. I knew I disappointed my family and I also knew that everyone would know that I had sex. I felt like a disgrace and I knew I wouldn't be trusted to do anything for a long time. My parents decided I would get an abortion at five and half months pregnant. After that my whole little world seemed so dark.

I felt so much shame and guilt even though at that time I didn't know how to name those feelings. I felt like I lost the trust of my family and friends. I felt dirty and soiled. I don't know what happened after that, but it happened fast. I needed to hear that somebody loved me. I am not saying my family didn't, but that I needed to hear it and feel it. By this time I realized that I was making choices that my parents didn't like.

What I came to understand is that there was a void. There was something inside of me that needed to feel something. This grew stronger because of the guilt and shame I felt. I didn't know what I was supposed to do with all these things I was feeling and all this pain. I didn't know whom God was so I didn't know how to reach out to Him. So I did what I knew, which was to keep it all inside.

I often questioned why I was made like this. I didn't believe I was having a pity party, I just didn't have any answers nor did I know how to ask the questions. I realized I had a need that implied a lack that must be filled. It appeared that I was the only one that knew this and at age 14.

Words Of Encouragement

One of the things that helped me to get here and to share my story was the good; the bad and me learning who I am. I allowed God into my life and I looked to Him to show me what love really is because I related to both love and pain. I didn't believe I deserved the love that was given to me. Even if I did feel like I was indebted to anyone for showing me love. You can make receiving very difficult because you have to first believe you deserve to receive it. Learn who you are and trust the love in you and learn and grow.

What I know now is this was the foundation that my life was being built on. However God sits high and looks low:

In the beginning God created the heaven and the earth. 2 And the earth was without form, and void; and darkness was upon the face of the deep. And the Spirit of God moved upon the face of the waters. Genesis 1:1-2

This scripture is important to me because I believe that God created everything and everyone. He created everyone having a void in his or her hearts and that let me know that I was not alone. This helped me to understand that the void I was feeling was so much deeper inside of me.

CHAPTER THREE
RUNNING INTO THE HANDS OF SATAN

*"You will face your greatest opposition when
you are closest to your biggest miracle."*
Shannon L. Alder

I started going back to school after the abortion. I remember one day this man showed up at the bus stop that I was waiting at. It's like he came out of nowhere. He began to say things to me like *"You're fine, can I get your number?" "You sure are cute."* Those words were like food to my soul. I was looking for anyone or anything that would make me feel better than what I was feeling. This man slid in like a snake and whispered things to me and I believed them. I was still trying to fill this void that had grown bigger because of guilt and shame.

This same man began to call me and I would sneak away and talk to him. He began to tell me he liked me a lot and he would take care of me. Even if it wasn't true, I believed it. I had to get away from the mess I created. So I ran away from home at age 14. Soon after running away, I discovered the life of prostitution. I shut down all feelings and emotions and like a child; I did whatever I was told. After several attempts of my family trying to rescue me, I continued to return to prostitution. What I began to think of as *The Life*.

I remember my brother coming to Portland after getting news I was headed there. I believe I was cramping the other ladies style because I was so young, which brought extra heat to *the track*. When I got to Portland my brother was standing on *Union Street*; this was *the track* where girls worked. I soon left for another state.

Prior to coming to Portland my parents would comb the streets of Seattle every night looking for me. The other ladies would let me know. I often had to work in areas that were not known for girls to work. However, I had already had a taste of *The Life*. How could I go back? I knew I would've just added one more thing to the list of bad choices. This was the worst. I was now a prostitute, better known as a hoe.

After a few years my family came to realize that I was not coming back. I worried my family for so many years. They didn't know if I was dead or alive. This lifestyle and everything that goes along with it carried on for 12 years. I was beaten with hot clothes hangers and I prostituted every day of the week. I never learned anything that would be useful outside of prostitution. I was traveling from state to state but never accomplished anything.

There were several occasions where my life almost ended. It is only by the grace of God that I am still here. I remember one time I was on *the track* and I remember getting hit so hard in my face, that I had two black eyes and a broken nose because I was talking to someone else and I had no money to give. I still continue to work even after that.

I went to Denver and soon after I became pregnant. Despite the growing life inside of me, I continued to work until I went into labor. When I was in labor I was left without a place to bring my baby home too. One of my friends and his lady let me stay at their place while I went to work to make enough money to get back to Seattle.

This would be the first time my family would have seen me in 4 years and now I was coming home with a baby.

I Swore

It was January of 1980 when I arrived back in Seattle. There was so much snow. Because the cab could not drive through the snow to my parents' house, I had to walk four blocks with my newborn baby. I was so disconnected, that I didn't even know my parents were separated. After finding out about my parents and even having my baby, I felt sad an even more disconnected. I had sworn I was done. Besides, the only thing that I learned was fear and loyalty; which was strange because the people I was around had none. It didn't take long before I broke my promise to myself and went back to prostitution. I began to travel again and I would leave my baby girl Tasha with her grandmother.

After a few months I found out that my babies grandmother was seeking custody of my child because of my lifestyle. I can remember sending extra money to her, however there was still consequences for the choice I made, when I left her.

When I found out I was being summoned to court, I came to Seattle and did whatever I needed to get my baby. I decided that I was not leaving her anymore. Three years later I had another baby girl and pretty much knew I was definitely going to stay in Seattle.

I wasn't quite sure what this meant for me or what it was going to look like. I knew I had to provide for my children and get a place for us to live. What I hadn't figured out was how I was going to do it. I never had my own apartment before. During all these years of prostitution I never had a place to live other than motels. Furthermore, I was never taught anything about how to save or manage money. Everything I had I gave away; my body, my mind my feelings, my heart, and my emotions.

The best thing that came out of it all was my two beautiful daughters. I saw this as beautiful because I learned that everything that God creates is beautiful when he gives it life.

As I got older I began to get even more tired of *The Life*. At this point drugs began to come on the scene. I began to wonder why there was never any money. There was always two or three of us working the streets, yet we were always broke. It was then that I was introduced to drugs. I continued to work *the track* so that I could not only live, but also live to get high.

CHAPTER FOUR
IF NOTHING CHANGES

*"Everyone thinks of changing the world, but
no one thinks of changing himself."*
Leo Tolstoy

While all this is going on in my life, I knew that my sister, Brenda, had gotten saved. Meaning that she had accepted Jesus Christ as her Lord and Savior and she began to go to church. God began to change her life. I also knew that she was praying for me because I noticed that she was now different with me.

When I made the choice to runaway from home and to start prostituting, my family was angry with me because they didn't understand why I would make decisions that would ruin my life. But my sister was always an encourager and had a positive outlook on things. So when God deposited His spirit in her, she displayed even more love and affection without any judgment.

My sister would frequently invite me to church. And when I would come into town she would ask me if I was ok; always warning me to be careful and telling me how much she loved me. When my girls were 3 and 5 I decided I didn't want to leave them or continue to travel all over with them. As I began to settle in Seattle I started getting tired of the lifestyle for several different reasons. All the money was going toward drugs and hotels when myself and my babies weren't staying at their grandmothers. I needed a place for my children and me. I continued working the streets. Being threatened made it impossible to leave and if I did try, I would get beat near to death.

I applied for housing and continued to work the streets. Drugs were a huge part of my lifestyle now. I finally got a place and I was going to work while he bought girls over to my house to have sex and get high. I was so tired.

I remember having to turn myself in to do thirty days in jail. One of my friends and my *wife-in-laws* offered to take care of my girls. I knew they would be safe with her. On top of that, her and I had a good relationship.

When I went to jail I was scared to leave the life style because I knew there would be consequences. It was all I knew. I got on my knees and began to pray in my cell for God to give me the courage to leave and not have any fear. When it was time for me to get released, I felt different. When my ride came to pick me up I got in that car and I looked at the person I knew God had answered my prayers. There was nothing. There was no fear, no love, nothing. When I arrived home the person that gave me a ride left and told me they would be back to take me to work. I was so glad to see my kids. I decided to packed my kids some clothes and I left my house. I found a safe place that didn't remind me of my lifestyle.

After I had left my house I still had to figure out how I was going to provide for myself and my children. I began to look for a job and I started working. I told myself again I was done with, that lifestyle and relationships, But the void in my life was still there along with my drug habit. During the time I was gone away from my house it was vandalized

When I was in that jail cell, I wish I would have known that praying for deliverance from drugs, unhealthy relationships, strong holds and healing would work because I would have prayed for that too. As my children began to grow up, they suffered many things because of my choices. The little I knew about raising kids came from my parents. I knew nothing about finances and taking care of a house. My parents were good providers and they took care of everything. I was too young when I ran away to get the knowledge of how they did it.

The Void

I still had this void within me; there was something that I needed. I thought if I got out of that bad relationship and stopped working the streets, then I would be okay. I began to struggle off and on with using drugs. This led me to use money that I needed for bills on drugs and that led me to hustle when I needed that money. I was still doing the same old thing, but instead of a man drugs became my pimp.

After a short while, when I was on one of my many short vacations to jail. This particular facility I resided was called *Knurf*. *Knurf* was an extension of A County Jail and a minimum-security facility that housed misdemeanors. At the time they housed men and women together and we could communicate, walk outside together, and sit together at meals. There I met a different kind of man. His character was different from what I was familiar with. He was a gentleman and had a different demeanor about himself. However, he wasn't a total square because he was locked up for driving offenses. We began to talk back and forth when he got out, and of course I started to like him because it appeared he didn't want anything from me. He was quite honest. He said he was a recovering addict but he was clean at this point. I didn't care because he was by far better than anything I had ever experienced.

The next season of life would be one I didn't expect. It would help me to start to see the issues and problems I had. Everybody thought that the relationship or the lifestyle I chose ruined my life, but that was just a Band-Aid that covered the issues I had deep inside of me. I was still trying to feel a void.

Words Of Encouragement

"Healing begins with understanding." - Bryan Stevenson

"When we attain an offence in our heart we filter everything through it. How I view my past relationships is the scope of the new ones " - John Beaver.

> 7 *Ever learning, and never able to come to the knowledge of the truth.* 2 Timothy 3:7

This is how I felt because I had not yet met truth. Even if I did during the several times I went to church I didn't open my heart up to receive it. Part of my journey of how I got here was being tired of the things that didn't appear to be working. How I learned they weren't working is by slowly opening my heart and my ears to understand and to listen.

CHAPTER FIVE
BEEN ON THIS MOUNTAIN LONG ENOUGH

"I thought climbing the Devil's Thumb would fix all that was wrong with my life. In the end, of course, it changed almost nothing. But I came to appreciate that mountains make poor receptacles for dreams."
Jon Krakauer

The young man in jail that I met we soon began to date. I don't know if I had ever been on a real date before. I began to like him more when I realized he didn't want anything from me. I believed that if I loved someone I had to prove it by giving them money. This man was different. I began to fall in love with him. At least from my understanding of what love was. He was a recovering addict and had been clean for a while. I didn't care because he treated me well. I lived in my house for about three more years while we dated. After a while things began to change.

His whole demeanor was off. I remember he used to go into the bathroom and he spent a lot of time in there. I recalled in the last days of my relationship with my children's father (my pimp), we had a little apartment off of *Madison Street* and he would do the same things. He would go into the bathroom for long periods and come out dripping with sweat. I began to ask him what he was doing and I wasn't totally dumb to the signs of drug use. However, all I knew about was crack cocaine and I didn't smell any crack so I didn't fully believe he was doing drugs. I finally asked my knew boyfriend if he was using drugs and he told me he was shooting cocaine into his veins; he began to do it in front of me.

Pretty soon he started leaving and not coming around as much. We were no longer doing the things we used to do. I began to get sad because I knew drugs were keeping him away. I wanted to know what he liked about it so much. My curiosity prompted me to want to try it too. He obliged me. To me this was just one more choice added to my list of bad ones.

We stayed together using off and on. Our date nights became drug runs and us hustling to get more drugs. After about three years, I moved out of my house and moved in with him and his mother. She had a stroke so he lived in and took care of her. I soon learned he was a mama's boy and I loved him for that. I enrolled my kids in school out there. I was still using drugs and acting as if we were living a normal life. I also began to help him care for his mom.

After a year of moving in we got married. At the time I didn't even understand what the covenants of marriage meant. My wedding was the saddest wedding I had ever seen. The preacher came to the house and read us our vows while the kids were running around; that was it. The family wasn't too keen on us getting married. They all thought that I just wanted his money. Really I just wanted a man. I just wanted someone who loved me. After we were married nothing really changed. He began to leave even more than before. Leaving me to care for his mom. I soon found out he was using heroin now. So I started using heroin too in hopes that he would stay home.

Selfishness

His mom had another stroke and needed 24-hour care. We took care of her and our habit. During this time my daughters were growing up. They were right there to experience all of this dysfunction. My children suffered from broken promises, neglect, and lies. They never had the necessities they needed because I was spending all of my money on drugs. Most of all, they were suffering from not receiving love and affection.

They were never told how beautiful and wonderful they were; they watched me chase after relationships and drugs; my girls didn't have a chance. My addiction got so bad that I began shooting drugs in my neck. Everything I did revolved around getting money to get drugs and pleasing my husband. After a while it didn't matter. It became all about me. I stayed in this marriage for 11 years after going in and out of jail and to prison twice.

His mom was moved to an adult family home and died six months later. We then moved to an apartment complex where most of my family members lived. Still addicted, I managed to get a job. We looked for a bigger place during this time and my daughter was starting to act out. I didn't know how to handle it because I was still in my addiction.

At age 14 she ended up running away just as I did. My youngest daughter who was still with me, I found that she was pregnant. I knew for sure that I was not going to make her have an abortion. Not because I didn't believe in them because I had two of my own. It was something inside of me that felt it would be wrong.

My next fear was telling my family about the pregnancy. How was my baby going to deal with this? As time went on she gave birth to a beautiful baby girl. It was the saddest experience watching my baby give birth to a baby. One thing I was grateful for was her best friend who stood by her until the end. That was so important. My daughter continued to go to school while she lived with me and I helped her with my grandchild. I was still working and addicted. I also managed to have criminal cases hanging over my head. It got so bad that we had to move again. Within the next few years, I went to prison. The kids were here and there. Staying with different family members. My oldest daughter had a baby 5 months after my youngest. I had two beautiful grandchildren.

I repeated the cycle of using and jail for a couple of years. When I got out of prison my husband managed to keep the apartment that we got before I went to prison and he had stopped using. I was gone for less than a year. Right away, I knew I needed to get a job. I had no desire to use. This was right around Christmas time and I remember wanting to get a Christmas tree for my grandkids. My husband said we couldn't afford it. I remember saying, *"We can't afford a Charlie brown tree?"* So to find a job I went. While I was coming from and interview, I stopped downtown and what I knew best kicked in. I hustled for the money and I got the Christmas tree.

My husband and I began to grow apart and he began to use again. We separated and I continued to work. Eventually, I started using cocaine again; neglecting my bills. This was another time I had to move. I ended up getting charges filed on me from an old case so I had to go back to prison.

CHAPTER SIX
IF I COULD ONLY GET A JOB

*"If to love each other is the job,
then the happy life is the salary."*
Toba Beta

This time when I was released from prison, my daughter had gotten an apartment in the central area. I moved in with my youngest daughter. I began to work and help her take care of my grandbaby. I was clean for a while, and then I started using drugs off and on. I started talking to someone I was interested in. This person was in a relationship with several girls, but it didn't bother me because I validated that it was okay in my mind.

I got a good job and worked really hard. I even started making plans to buy my own home. During this time the unit we lived in was right next door to a church. I remember on Sundays watching the people go in and out. There was something about them. They looked so happy. I finally went over to attend then I began to go more and more. At that time, I knew I didn't want to use drugs any more so I started taking pills. That's when I got turned on to *China White;*. *China White* is a different form of heroin that I could snort.

It felt like whenever I went through anything emotional I dealt with it through drugs. The only thing about this drug is that you would get sick if you didn't have it and that's something I surely couldn't manage. So I tried rehab. I got in a program at the *Evergreen Treatment Center (Methadone Clinic)*. To get off drugs they gave us a liquid dose of synthetic heroin every day. This program was put in place with the hopes of cutting the crime rate down. I didn't like it and I stopped going and I tried to kick my addiction myself. I started going to church more and more. I did manage to purchase my own home and buy a new car. I remember my pastor saying so clearly, *"Sis Smiley stay close to the church."* This was because the place I was moving to was far away from the central area. He said this as if he could see something I could not. I simply replied *"I will Pastor."*

During the time I was really trying to stay clean. I had accumulated more bills. I began to try and sell while working. All while trying to learn more about who God is.

Soon after I moved I began to go to church less and less. My addiction kicked back in. I was trying to hide it from the man I was with but it caused me to use more. I was wearing a mask. This was the lowest I had ever been. I was in such a dark state.

I never heard black people talk about depression in our culture so at the time I was unable to name my experience. But if I would've known then what I now know I would say that I was definitely In a state of depression. For months I avoided contact with everybody. I stopped working too. The position I held was seasonal. I didn't get fired, I just never went back after my time off. I was still lying about my drug use to the man I was seeing.

I remember one night I was driving and I blacked out. I don't know how long I had been driving north on I-5. When I came to my senses I was still on the road.

I know God had His angels protecting me because I didn't kill anyone or myself. Soon after that, I ended up getting a case. I was out on bond and missed my court date. I knew when I finally went to court I was going to have to do some time. So I just rode it out until the end and when it finally reached that point, I turned myself in. I knew in that moment that if I didn't go to jail, I was going to die or do something that was going cause me to face an even longer sentence; longer than what I was already facing which was 60 months.

In June 2007, I turned myself in to King County Jail leaving all the mess that I had created behind. The voice in my head was saying, *"Look what you did now you're going to just leave? You need to clean this mess up!"* I felt like a coward. Surely I am the *bad bitch* I was told I was all these years. I had the evidence to prove it. Staying with a man that beat me and remaining faithful to him proved something. Doing whatever things that were asked of me shaped my identity. I was down for whatever. I was never the type to *conk out*. Those words *conk out*, made me feel like I failed. In my mind that was the worst thing. I'd asked myself *how could I fail at this too?*

In June, I finally conked out. Everything in me was tired. One thing I know about myself is that I take responsibility for my own choices. No matter what I experienced in life, no matter how bad people treated me. I knew I had to turn myself in. I believe it comes from a place of selflessness. I use to think I was the most selfless person because all I did for other people. I was always trying to please them. God later showed me that I was the most selfish person.

I did not think about anybody or anything but myself all the way up to the time of turning myself in to King County Jail. Trying to fill that void allowed me to forget about everybody else's void; including my children and grandchildren. The truth is I didn't know how to even start filling it. I needed something better than what I knew and was taught. Because what I knew was not working for me. I knew when I went to jail that I needed to give my life to Christ. And that's what I did.

My behavior or lifestyle went on for 30 years. God began to show Himself in merciless ways to me. There was no doubt in my mind that in order for me to live, I needed Christ to lead, guide, teach, and heal me. The old me would have to die. I was not sure of what that meant at the time. I knew that everything I had tried leading up to this moment had not worked. I was so broken and had caused other lives to be broken. I committed my time in jail and prison to Him.

Words Of Encouragement

Strongholds create a set pattern of recovering through which all incoming information is processed. Although they were originally designed for protection they have become a source of torment and distortion because they way against the knowledge of God.

I needed intimacy, honesty and healing. I knew it had to be something more. I just wanted to be cared for at the core of who I was. What I know for certain is for forgiveness to truly happen something has to die.

> 10 *Create in me a clean heart, O God; and renew a right spirit within me.* Psalm 51:10

CHAPTER SEVEN
TOTAL SURRENDER

*"You cannot fulfill God's purposes for your
life while focusing on your own plans."*
Rick Warren

As I began the journey in jail headed to prison, I wanted to focus on God changing my life because I had made such a mess of it. As I look back, I know that God has a sense of humor.

My roommate was a young lady and was a devout Christian. She also was the grandmother of my niece's grandchild. My oldest brother and her shared the same grandchild. I learned a lot from this amazing lady. We were at the King County Regional Justice Center Jail in Kent, WA. I was housed there for 6 months before being sentenced and sent to prison. During this time there are three key people that came to visit me. One was my Pastor and his beautiful wife. I didn't call them they just came. I began to get cards from a few of their church mothers. My pastor just looked at me with those fatherly eyes and said, "*How you are sis Smiley?"* I replied, *"I am fine Pastor. I have re- dedicated my life to God."* He said, *"we will see."* He would say how much the churched loved me and that everyone was praying for me. His beautiful wife has so much love and compassion. She loved me. I knew it because I felt no judgment. It was just what I needed in that moment. My Pastor brought me truth.

I never called for anyone to come see me or put money on my books; people would just do it. It became clear to me that I was not the *bad bitch* that I thought I was all these years. I could not say it out loud, but through this visit God showed me that I was still a mess; I was still holding on. He showed me that I had not fully surrendered.

I began to pray for God to remove anything and anybody that was distracting me from Him. And that's just what he did. Even when I tried to not focus on the mess I made and all of the dysfunctional relationships, I just couldn't stop my mind from replaying the tape in my head that said I was not lovable. This was my second experience of God letting me know He was real.

So for the first time sitting in RJC I didn't mind being a *conk out*. I thank God I was brought to this point in my life. I was in so much despair and saw no hope within myself. I now see He could not work within me any other way.

When I was in county, I started praying and asking for God to give me tools that I could use to help me get stronger and draw me closer to Him. What I find funny is that before I came to jail I had a Gospel tape in my car with different artists on it. One of my favorite songs was a short altar call song by TD Jakes. It simply says, *"I surrender to thee my precious savior. I give everything to Jesus."* This became my song that he implanted in my soul, my heart, and spirit because He knew I would need to bellow these words out of my spirit.

On September 16, 2007, God filled me with His precious Holy Spirit in that Jail cell. On my knees he filled me and delivered me. I continued to ask God to consecrate me and set me apart to clean me from the inside out. I wanted to remove anything that was in the way.

When I was on my way to sentencing the jail guard placed me in a holding cell with other women waiting to go into the courtroom. As I was sitting I could smell that one of the ladies had heroin. I could smell it like a cake baking. I was nervous for my sentencing and I thought the dope would calm my nerves. I remember thinking that I wouldn't get sick because it's just one time.

Suddenly, I just began to praise God and tears began fall down my face because I knew God had His hand on me. He put an arm of protection around me. That day I chose not to use and that was definitely God.

Working On My Mind

There are so many times when God showed me His power and just how much he loved me during my time in county and even at my sentencing. As I moved on to the Washington Correctional Facility for Women, I began to get my mind focused on whatever God had for me. One of the biggest things was really learning to trust God because of the strong holds that had been created in my life. I do believe I was trusting God for healing and deliverance, however my thoughts kept going against the positive things I was trying to focus on.

For the most part, I felt I was in tune to whatever God was doing. I was so humble; God was trying to move me to a different facility while I was trying to stay where I was at because I was comfortable. Of course, He won.

Being in this place God was able to do such amazing work on me beyond belief. He showed me His Glory and He set me free in my mind. He let me know that I am capable of achieving anything in life if I keep Him first. He showed me that He would give me the desires of my heart even in the hard places, even in prison. He reached me right inside of there. His Glory was what did it.

This is what I experienced; all this while I am locked up, yet free. It was too much I thought. God was showing me all of His power and Glory. He let me know that He can reach me anywhere.

I was at Mission Creek Correctional Facility, an extension of WCCW (Minimum Security). Part of being there you were assigned to a work crew. I was assigned to *Cancer Retreat Place* and *St. Andrews House*. There was no doubt in my mind that God placed me there to continue to show me who He is.

While I was there I stood on the mountain of that beautiful resort. I saw eagles and deer frequently. Planted were the most beautiful flowers and we picked fresh fruit right off the branches. You could look out at the water. We were even served fresh oysters right out of the sea.

During my stay I took a college course in office management and I received my GED. When we graduated, out of all the ladies that completed the office management class and GED, I was chosen to be the Keynote speaker. My teacher was so proud of me. We were able to invite our family. I decided to extend the invitation to my sister and my mom. They agreed to come, but at the last minute they called and said they were going to be late and might not make it. As soon as I got up to speak they walked in. They were lucky; normally if you're late you can't come in.

This was first time I saw my mother cry and the first time I remember hugging her. This was the first time in my life that I felt like my mom was proud of me and it didn't matter that I was in prison. That was the most important thing for me in that moment. Even as I think back on how I got here, I knew God was doing all these things.

CHAPTER EIGHT
IT'S TIME

"You can have it all. Just not all at once."
Oprah Winfrey

As I was preparing for my release, I realized that I needed a release address. My sister told me that the Seattle Union Gospel Mission was building a new facility. She went to enquire about it and got the information. I submitted the address to the Department of Corrections and they denied it because they were listed as a shelter. So I submitted my mother's address and it was approved. I was released and then life began.

When I was locked up I wrote my mom a letter apologizing for everything I had done; every heartache and every tear I caused. When I was at my mom's I immediately realized there's were a lot of issues that were deeply rooted. I found myself feeling the need to get busy looking for a job and enrolling in school. That was my plan. What I remembered was my past pattern of getting out and starting over. That was my regular routine. However this time I was on three years DOC. It meant if I violated the law I would go back and finish the three-year sentence with no exceptions.

I remember my sister contacting me asking if I'd ever connected with Hope Place. Ms. Johnny was the program director at the time. I responded no and that they denied the address. My sister suggested that I should call her anyway and go see it. So I did.

I scheduled an appointment and I went to Hope Place to meet with Ms. Johnny and lay out my plans. She just looked. Finally she said if I was interested in doing this program I wouldn't be able to attend school or work the first year. I thought *"Lord have mercy!"*

She could tell by my facial expression that I was disappointed. She said, *"Let those that have ears hear."* After that I told her that I would love to be here however I still had the one issue. DOC.

I called them right away and said I need to get into Hope Place. To my surprise my probation officer said okay! That was God at work. He wanted me to see the issues I still had with my mom and the pattern that I always returned to. What God showed me is that he had not even begun to do the work he needed to do in me.

The next day I moved in and cried when I looked out my room window and saw fireworks. I took it as a sign of God showing me that he was pleased with me. The classes they offered dealt with healing brokenness, addictions, trauma, and past pain. I felt safe there. There were boundaries set and bible studies that help you to know who God is and develop a deeper relationship. These are things that I didn't deal with when I was locked up. God showed me a lot about whom I was. My plan now changed from mine to His.

There are four major events that happened while I was at Hope Place. These events, I believed change me in some form or another.

After being in the program for 4 or 5 months, I knew my daughters were struggling and therefore my grandkids were struggling too. I asked if I could have my granddaughter come live with me. Now this was tough because Hope Place didn't have grandchildren, only women with their own children. I knew they needed me so if they said no I don't think I would have stayed. I prayed and they said yes. My daughter agreed that I could keep her for a while.

Soon after, my other granddaughter needed to be with me as well. I prayed and God answered. Now I had two of my oldest grandkids. I willed to do my best. I was grateful that God gave me the opportunity to be in my granddaughter's lives in a positive way. They had seen so much dysfunction. They weren't going to have a chance. I also had the opportunity to have my grandson with me for a short while there at Hope Place.

My daughters did the best they could with what they knew. I prayed that the viscous cycle and generational curse would be broken in my family. This was God saying, *"I am here."* God showed me myself through my grandchildren, which was so hurtful at times.

I didn't know how to be a parent or a grandparent. Love and affection had to be taught to me but I first had to love myself. I could say I love God, but what about me? When God showed himself to me I still had relationship issues and a codependency issue. It was because I was still trying to fill that void. I was trying to get approval from man. I valued what they thought about me. I desired to be sexually attractive because it made me feel like I was worth something. So here I was almost half a year in the program and I still had all these issues.

I knew in many ways I was not honoring God. Yet I was still praying for him to help me. The one thing I did commit to was putting my grandkids needs before my own. I believe that's why I had so many struggles. Maybe it was because I didn't totally keep God first. That's the message I wanted my family, church, my community I lived in to see. Most of all I wanted to believe in it for myself.

Refreshed

I went to a retreat that was hosted by *Tabernacle Missionary Baptist Church* called *The Love Retreat at Ocean Shores*. That was such a major life changing experience for me. That was God reminding me of who He was and it helped me to continue to stay focused on Him. I believe that at that retreat, God required an even deeper relationship with me. He also showed me that He loved me in spite of the struggles I continued to have. He promised me then at that ocean *"I will never leave you or forsake you."* I went to that retreat two years in a row.

My other life changing experience was through a bible study called *Healing Hearts*. Through that study God showed me that nothing is hidden to him. He desires the most inward parts. I started communing with Him in truth and transparency. One of my issues was sex and masturbation. Something that we didn't talk about in the program. I was able to talk about these things in *Healing Hearts*. I knew that I needed to confess my sin not only to God, but also to another believer that would pray for me and speak truth and encouragement.

Since my grandkids were doing so well, I stayed another year doing a discipleship program and I graduated. I was so glad when it was time for me to move forward and God opened the door so I could be employed at *The Mission at Hope Place*.

I continued to attend the church I was going to before I went to prison. I simply loved my church family. I have had many struggles but my good outweighs my bad. Both of my granddaughters are in college and doing well. God has a plan for their life.

The one thing I am grateful for that He has deposited in me is the ability to never give up. I know that God is real. I have hurt many people in my lifetime and I truly apologize to anyone I have hurt or offended. I need the umbrella of grace.

God has equipped me to share this little piece of my life because it truly displays all His glory and what he will do if we trust Him and dedicate our life to Him. I have many struggles; what's different now is I have an advocate that's available any time of the day or night to hear my cry and wipe my tears. What that does is give me peace. A peace that only he can give and it surpasses all understanding while I am in the storms. As I write this book, I am smiling because there is so much that I am going through.

What He has whispered and reminded me of is to totally surrender to what He requires. I know the reason I keep going around the same mountains. If you take anything away from this book, just know that He loves you more than anything you can ever imagine. It's called *Agape Love* and it's unconditional. It's the love that God sheds abroad in our hearts. It's not based on performance or even if it's returned or not because it's unconditional.

It's no mistake that you're reading these words. God has a plan for your life and it's beyond anything you can imagine. Trust Him. Every one of us have a void placed within us. That's the way God designed us so that we would seek him. What I know for sure today is that God is the only one that can fill that void. As I lean onto Him daily, He reminds me of this very thing. When I slip and fall it gets easier and easier to get back up and continue to trust Him.

Words Of Encouragement

> *"I am more than the worst thing I have ever done. You can find redemption in the most unexpected places." - Bryan Stevenson*

Prayer from "Battle Plan for Prayer" By Stephen Kendrick

"Father in heaven I praise your wonderful name. Lord it's holy and to be honored. I worship you as my God and ask that you glorify yourself in my life. Search me and cleanse me of anything that displeases you. Forgive me as I forgive others. Thank you for your provision, protection and faithfulness in my life. Thank you for inviting me into your presence daily. Teach me to pray. Oh Lord Train me to joyfully bow in worship, to freely confess all sin. I thank you with a humble heart, praying this for them and also myself and those closest to me. All to your Glory In Jesus name I pray Amen. Be Blessed."

CHAPTER NINE
TRANSPARENCY

"Truth never damages a cause that is just."
Mahatma Gandhi

    I believe there is a healing that comes when you are transparent and walk in humility. This whole journey *"How Did I Get Here"* I believe was about me learning who I am. I am in a position of leadership in my professional life and in my personal life. I believe we all have roles of leadership. I have to know who I am to be able to lead. All of my life I have been a follower. Because of that, it's been hard for me to trust my ability to lead at times. One thing that I began to notice about myself is that I have a natural gift and talent in me to take charge and to be a servant. I am so grateful for that part of my character. I simply love to serve and in many different arenas. What I know for certain is I can't be a good leader if I am not able to follow.

    I have had some amazing experiences in the last five years of my life. I have had some really challenging experiences that have forced me to make decisions that would affect not only my life but also the lives of grandchildren. Today I am certain that I made the right decisions. For once in my life I was not selfish thinking only of myself. I was given grace and a second opportunity to be a part of my family's life in a positive way. My grandchildren suffered and experienced some things that were passed down from generations in our family.

What God allowed me is a second chance to be part of these young kids lives as their grandmother and influence them in a positive way. In such a way that they would know who Christ is. I pray that they desire to have a relationship with Him. I wanted them to have a chance at life and be loved unconditionally.

During a season of my life, it was not easy to understand unconditional love because things that I had to give to them, I didn't quite know how. I was learning as I was put in position to do it. Yet I was still fighting this battle in my mind and in my heart about my own selfish desires to be in a relationship.

Today I am grateful and I do realize it was a blessing to be given another chance to lead in such a positive away after all I experienced. I also began to realize that I had to start at home with family and me. I have two amazing daughters. I love them and I know that they love me. I use to believe that things will just go away once I started making the right choices and began to live life right according to God. In my heart I know it doesn't just go away. There is still unfinished business that I have with my family. I know that there are things that they would like to share with me and they may not know how. I was a very selfish person putting my needs before theirs.

I also know that God is helping me to create and environment that will make them feel safe enough to share whatever pains and heartaches they have so that they can receive healing. My granddaughters have been a huge part of my growth as a person. What I have learned in this season of my life is that I would have continued to go around that same mountain if I didn't totally surrender to God and change some things.

I have grown and I have been delivered. I no longer walk in fear or shame. I know for certain that I can't live my life apart from God. I can't be effective living a double life. The great Maya Angelou said *"When you know better you do better."* That simple. It's good for my soul to speak truth and to walk in transparency. There may be things that people don't agree with, however everyone looks at life through a different lens and the lens that I was looking through were shaped by the environment I was in.

One thing I do today is I count all of my joy. In the Bible, in the book of James, it talks about counting it all joy. I love that there is nothing that's not covered in the Word of God. Today my two amazing daughters love me they have forgiven me; I am working on being a better mom for them. They gave me the opportunity to really be part of my two oldest granddaughters lives… and they are amazing! God has amazing plans for their lives and he has blessed them in so many ways.

I have been blessed to work in and organization where we can freely worship Christ and share the Word. I have had many challenges along the way. However, God never changes. He is the same yesterday, today, and forevermore. I am humbly grateful. My vision and my dream is to own and operate a home for young girls fleeing sex trafficking and Domestic Violence.

When I look back over my life and being in those hard places, I remember wanting to go someplace safe and receive love and not condemnation. For many years it was hard for me to ask for things that I wanted because I never felt like I deserved anything. God said he would give us the desires of our heart if we serve Him and live our life for Him honoring Him. There are a lot of blessings that I have hindered because of my disobedience. I pray and ask God for forgiveness; he clearly shows me myself when that happens.

There have been so many tears I have cried over the years. I will never forget because they have become part of my testimony. God has worked something in me and out of me. I know that his purpose for my life and the life of everyone reading this is to encourage someone and to bring life out of death; freedom out of bondage; and turn darkness into light. The reality is I could have been dead a long time ago because of the choices that I made. From the beginning of my story to the end I speak my truth. I pray that it causes no one any pain. As I went through this process I cried because I am so grateful that I am able to share my story today.

CHAPTER TEN
YOU HAVE TO ENCOURAGE YOURSELF SOMETIMES

"If thousand people say you can't, and you alone believe you can, you will make it happen! But if million people say you can, and you alone believe you can't, you can't make it happen. It all depends on you!"
Israelmore Ayivor

One of the things that have helped me in my journey is words of encouragement. There are words that make me feel good and words that make me feel bad. Sometimes people know just what to say to make you feel bad about yourself. I still have my struggles when it comes to relationships. I am not where I would like to be, yet I am definitely not where I used to be. I thank God for His grace, mercy, and forgiveness. Every day I ask God to show me myself. Everything starts within me. I am responsible for my reaction to every situation. Whether be it good or bad ones.

I love Joyce Myers' Devotional Book, "Battle Field of the Mind." This book is one of the tools I use because it shows me myself. Sometimes I get out of character, but mostly in my mind. I would have a conversation going on in my head. This is very dangerous because whatever the things we think on will control us. I challenged myself to read and listen to things that are positive and that speak truth. I had to be able to identify a lie from the truth. One might think that's easy, however for some it is not.

When you have been told lies for years and you relate pain to love, it's hard to break those false belief patterns. What I learned is that I had to replace my negative thought patterns with positive thoughts. Some of the things I read in God's word are that I am beautifully and wonderfully made. I am set a part, I am a new creation in Christ Jesus, I am whole and complete, and I am set free! But one of my all-time favorites is "Greater is He that is in me than he that is in the world." I would read this, meditate on his words, and ask God to reveal His truth to me.

This didn't come naturally, I didn't just wake up and do it. I had to surrender to God and ask Him to help me because I could not do it. I tried a million times on my own. I broke about a million promises to God only to wander back to him. What God placed on my heart was first to trust him. Once I started doing that I would begin to search for different scriptures that applied to what I was feeling or when someone would speak an encouraging word to me about whatever I was experiencing. I was convinced that God sees and He cares about the smallest details in my life.

I learned that when a go through something, and I am trying to stop doing something that's not pleasing to God, or when I think I have gotten through this thing; God will show me that I have still not surrendered. There have been times where I truly believed in my heart that I would not do this or that again. No sooner than the opportunity presents itself I am saying "How Did I Get Here?" The encouraging thing about God is that He promises in His Word that He will never leave us or forsake us. I understand today that it's my choice of how long and how many times I want to go around the mountain. What's scary is that every time around it gets worse and worse. The negative self-talk will say it will be different. My own selfishness will have me ignore my feelings and thoughts.

Another encouraging thing about this is God sees and He searches our hearts. It took me a while to really understand this. I didn't need to hide anything from God because He already knows everything. This allowed me to be so open and transparent my soul literally cries out to Him. This made my relationship with Him more intimate. I believe that it grieves Gods heart when I struggle; especially when He always makes away of escape out of every situation. Even if it's me whispering, "Lord I trust you" when I couldn't do anything else. I love reading materials that speak truth about an experience. Somehow you can tell that it's truth. You often relate to the same kind of situation.

When I talk about my shortcomings, I always try and share the lesson I learned from it so that the message becomes and encouraging one. There are areas that I struggle in and will continue to because I am human. I do inspire to change

How Did I Get Here?

anything that's not pleasing to God. I have grown so much in the last few years.

As I look back on my journey through life, I learned that humility and transparency is key. I learned that I had to be willing to be quiet and listen. I learned not to be scared to open my mouth and speak my truth. And not fear that someone would dislike me for it. This was very challenging for me. So I would say one thing and operate in a whole other way. One more very important thing is reconciliation; it has to happen. People will not always receive your attempt to reconcile, but when you do it from your heart something changes inside of you. It's a state of humility.

This season in my life I am crossing over to my truth and my transparency. I am no longer walking in fear. I have experienced far worse things in my life than what will happen when I share my truth and shortcomings. I can now recognize strongholds that still try and creep up. I know that love does not hurt. I had to understand that we are all imperfect. I had to look through a lens of compassion and understanding. I was able to do that more and more when I started learning what it meant to love and to receive love in this world in which we live. How could I trust what was real? For me I had to measure my experiences by what I perceived as truth today.

I was reading one of my many journals I wrote when I was in prison. It's very encouraging for me to read them because it shows where I have grown and areas I still struggle in. One of the quotes I wrote, "I refuse to give up. I can't just quit! God whatever I got left, I am giving to YOU!"

The confidence that I have today helps me to avoid comparison. I understand today that God has sent people in and out of my life to exercise my faith and to develop my character. I learned that the people who treated me the worst in my journey, was preparing me for the best. I know that I am too important for the purpose of God to be destroyed by a situation that is only meant to give me character. No matter how painful or disappointed and devastated I felt. I now understand that the pain that was developed from rejection and failed relationships, I experienced because I was not at the end of myself. In a sense I was still trying to fill that void. I think about it like playing tug of war. In the bible, there's a scripture that Paul describes in Romans as a war going on in the inside of him. That's exactly what I was experiencing. I longed to do the right thing, but I kept messing up. I had not totally surrendered. Today I continue to pray this prayer that I wrote. I did not know then I would use it in this book. This is about transparency.

There is therefore now no condemnation to them, which are in Christ Jesus, who walk not after the flesh, but after the Spirit. Romans 8:1

This is my payer for guidance and to totally surrender:

Lord, I ask for forgiveness for any and everyone I have hurt with my actions with my words or with my thoughts. I need forgiveness from lying, fornication, adultery, stealing, and disobedience. Lord please forgive me and help me to salvage any relationships I had with people that I borrowed money from and was not able to pay back when promised. Lord help me to put you first in every situation and area of my life.

Lord, help me to hunger and thirst after you. Help me to fast and pray. Lord, help me to become a good steward over every nickel, dime, or penny you bless me with. I have made a mess over my finances; help me to start honoring you with my first fruit. Lord I give you all of me and if there is anything I am holding back please reveal it to me so that I may surrender. Lord help me to hold no anger or resentment towards anyone; please release any strongholds the enemy thinks he has victory of over my family and myself. Lord most of all create in me a clean heart and renew a right spirit within me. Amen.

My first thought before writing this was that the minute someone reads this someone would automatically begin to analyze the words I used. I thought about that before I wrote this personal prayer of mine. I thought about what would people think about my character? Would my fellow co-workers think I am a Christian that represents the very character of Christ? I know for certain that my Lord and Savior searches our very hearts and He desires that I seek him in spirit and in truth. I know that I can't continue to go around the same mountain; there has to be a change! And change is what I desire and what I have done. I no longer struggle with certain things and I am going to keep seeking God who is the author and the perfectionist of my fate. I have confidence in Him. He has chosen me and has equipped me to come boldly before the throne of grace.

CONCLUSION

LUKE 22:31-32

31 And the Lord said, Simon, Simon, behold, Satan hath desired to have you, that he may sift you as wheat:
32 But I have prayed for thee, that thy faith fail not: and when thou art converted, strengthen thy brethren.
PRAISE GOD!

This is one of my favorite scriptures because God is showing me that I am not alone and he knows and sees everything. Secondly, I notice He says if you are strengthened come back and help your brother.

During most of my life I made foolish choices for many different reasons, however no matter the reason; there's always a consequence to our choices; the good ones and bad ones. As I began to know who God is and believe that He loves me and that my life is not going to be complete without His guidance and direction, I have a peace that He has given me.

When I am faced with challenges such as loneness and finances, these two are my biggest struggles, I go to Him and when I listen to His word concerning these things I receive peace. When I choose to do things my own way and not trust him things go all bad and I have to travel around that mountain all over again. I have learned that loneliness is a state of mind, so it's very important that I begin to retrain and refocus my thinking.

Strongholds are real. When you have been taught certain things for many years, you begin to believe them and then you begin to operate through that belief system. For many years, I was told I was worthless, a hoe, a piece of shit; that I was a bitch, a tramp, and no one would want me. For a while, I believed that because the way I was treated. A poet once wrote *"Treat a man as he appears to be and you make him worse, but treat a man as if what he could potentially be and you make him what he should be."* It became clear to me after reading a lot of profound words of Pastor and author TD Jakes, that the reason I kept attracting certain type of men was because the same issues I had they also had. Even though they appeared to be strong and have control, they had the same void I had and was just as lost as I was. Because I came into that knowledge, God began to work on my heart for forgiveness. The word of God requires forgiving if we want to receive healing for ourselves.

When someone hurts you or breaks your heart, you have to forgive them so that they don't continue to have power over you. You will be free and God can complete the work that He has started in you.

Something has to die before forgiveness can happen. I believe it's hard because how do you correct something as slippery as a feeling?

What I know for sure is that this season of my life is a part of my destiny. God is birthing something great in me for His glory not for man nor women, but Him alone. God desires that we sing to the roof top about whom He is and His saving grace. This book is one of my many opportunities to share what God is doing in my life in hopes that you would be encouraged enough to seek Him. May God bless you and keep you.

This book was a very short read. I did this because I felt like giving you all of me at once was quite a bit. Also God did amazing things for me through the process of reading and writing. He's helping me process my thoughts as well as visually seeing what my mind is thinking in order to put it on paper. Everybody is rigged up different.

God desires us to share our amazing gifts and talents so that He may get the Glory. Although I once believed this was to personal and I couldn't even imagine sharing, there's a healing that God gives when we see what once was and what is now. Because of His love for us we believe in His amazing transforming power at work. I hope you enjoy and most of all I hope you allow God to fill your void.

Actionable

Freestyle what you believe and know for sure about yourself and your journey moving forward. Dream big we serve A God that owns everything.

> 11 *The voice of joy, and the voice of gladness, the voice of the bridegroom, and the voice of the bride, the voice of them that shall say, Praise the Lord of hosts: for the Lord is good; for his mercy endureth for ever: and of them that shall bring the sacrifice of praise into the house of the Lord. For I will cause to return the captivity of the land, as at the first, saith the Lord.* Jeremiah 33:11

> 6 *Be careful for nothing; but in every thing by prayer and supplication with thanksgiving let your requests be made known unto God.* Philippians 4:6

The peace of God, which transcends all understanding, will guard your hearts and your mind in Christ Jesus. He says that He will restore the years the locus has stolen. *What do you want restored?*

ABOUT THE AUTHOR

I am blessed even when I don't feel like I know that I am. I thank each and every person that has read this short book. I hope that it has encouraged you. I look forward to writing more as God leads as well doing motivational speaking. I am still employed with the Seattle Union Gospel Mission serving those in greatest need. I now have six beautiful grandchildren and they are truly a blessing. I am blessed to still have both of my parents; I now have 6 siblings left. I am not the baby girl anymore I have a beautiful little sister, Kaniea Smiley. I am learning to cherish family more. I have tons of nieces and nephews! So many that I don't even know them all. However, the one that is dear to my heart is Ms. Kyla Jackson. I love you and thank you for all of your support and your unconditional love. To my two dearest friends, Renee Reddick and Rachell Hill, I love you guys. Again to my dear sister Brenda and her husband they have encouraged through this entire process and my Pastors and his beautiful wife.

RESOURCES

www.waRecoveryHelpLine.org
www.Iwantrest.com
www.ywcaworks.org
www.suicidepreventionlifeline.org
Dial (211) crisis Clinic King County WA.
www.Ugm.org

Colossians 2:2-3
Psalms 18:19
Mathew 11:28-29
Philippians 4:6-7
Jeremiah 33:11

CPSIA information can be obtained
at www.ICGtesting.com
Printed in the USA
FFOW02n0925111116
29272FF